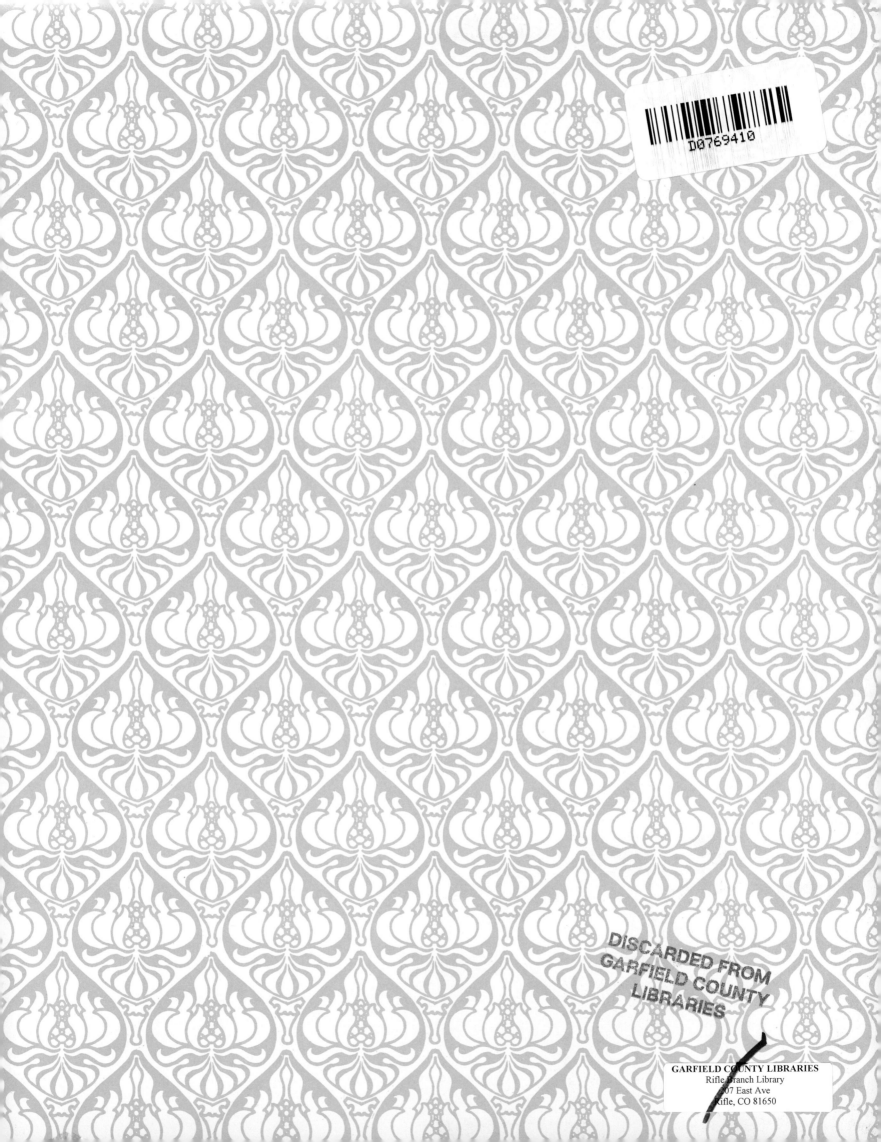

Corvina

BUDAPEST ANNO...

Picture photographs in the studio and outside

EDIFICES

LANDSCAPES

INTÉRIEURS

FACTORIES

GENRE SCENES

György Klösz
court photographer's art institution

FOR THE MOST PART, THE PHOTOGRAPHS
WERE TAKEN BY GYÖRGY KLÖSZ, THE REST BY HIS
KNOWN AND UNKNOWN CONTEMPORARIES.

Introduced by Lajos Mesterházi. Captions by Ervin Seenger
Translated by László T. András and Inez Kemenes
Pictures placed at the publishers' disposal by the Kiscell Museum of the Museum of Budapest History
Design by Gyula Mayer
© Text: Heirs of Lajos Mesterházi, 1979
ISBN 963 13 1830 3
2nd edition

Printed in Hungary, 1984
Révai Printing House, Budapest
and Offset and Card Printing House, Budapest
CO 2219-h-8488

Photography is not reckoned among the most significant of the major inventions that have shaped the modern world. Yet, without it there would be no film, the press would not be what it is, and a number of sciences would lack an important aid. This invention has created a new era in visual culture or, in brief, culture, since vision is a sense of unrivalled importance.

Photography gained ground in Hungary rather quickly. As early as the 1840s, a Hungarian invention helped to perfect Daguerre's process. Before long, photography became a representational art in its own right, and attained a not inconsiderable artistic level in this country. Hungary has given the world quite a few portrait photographers and photo reporters, including internationally recognized names such as Brassai and Capa.

György Klösz never enjoyed world-wide reputation. Nevertheless, he played a valuable part in the cultural history of Budapest. He set up his studio in 1867 in the city of Pest, his enterprise soon being joined by his son, who had graduated from the School of Graphic Art. Within a few decades, the photographic studio became one of the country's major graphic institutions and not much later a pioneering printing shop. György Klösz and Son Ltd. was still in existence up until the nationalization of printing presses in 1948. One might only wonder whether the founders were aware that they were not only inscribing their names in the history of Hungarian industry, but were also fulfilling an equally important mission with what were then known as *Ansichts* photographs, and that the glass plates made in their time for typographic multiplication and commercial purposes would one day be regarded as artistic and historical relics of great value. Just as Rudolf Alt's coloured lithographic plates have preserved for us the mid-19th century twin cities of Pest-Buda, so these photographs have done the same for the Budapest of the final two decades of the last and the beginning of the present century. The industrial entrepreneur has thus become an often quoted authority in the Hungarian press; in a sense we all see an epoch—and not just any epoch—of the capital city's history through his eyes.

The foundation year of 1867 is also a decisive date in Hungarian history. The lawlessness, the savage terror and the bureaucratic oppression that followed the overthrow of the 1848–1849 Revolution and War of Independence had ended. The Hungarian ruling classes and the House of Habsburg negotiated the *Ausgleich*, which brought about a dualist Austro-Hungarian Monarchy whose constitution, if not democratic, widened the road for middle-class development.

For example, the Compromise of 1867 made possible the administrative unification of the three sister cities of Buda, Óbuda and Pest in 1872–1873. It was a long overdue measure, since these cities had, in fact, grown together, and the revolutionary government of 1849 had already issued a decree on unification and the establishment of a united Budapest. After the fall of Hungary, however, Vienna did not want to see the rebellious city emerge as a rival, and to this end it kept up its administrative division as long as it could. The separation of the two cities of Buda and Pest had hampered systematic town development and modernization for decades. This obstacle was now removed. Between 1880 and 1905 the population of Budapest increased from four hundred thousand to one million. The Klösz photographs originated in this last quarter of a century, perpetuating the image of a suddenly expanding, adolescent city outgrowing itself almost by the day

The population explosion brought on tremendous changes in the city's external appearance and quality of life. Some of these were natural changes attendant upon the sudden increase in urban population; others were what we might term "unnatural" alterations, changes engineered by an act of the will, as it were. What I mean is that Napoleon III's brilliant architect, Haussmann, created in Paris the admirable model of the *fin de siècle* metropolis. Many European capitals endeavoured to emulate this model, Vienna among them, and Budapest followed the example of Vienna. The model being good, this would have been no serious mistake; the system of boulevards and avenues, as opposed to the chessboard model, had prevailed not by accident but design in Europe's large cities. But then a grotesque grimace kept disfiguring this visage on Budapest's countenance. The city did not or could not recognize its own character, it disastrously misunderstood its own past, and this dis-function of self-knowledge can be shown in the final analysis to reside in the ambiguities of the 1867 Compromise. Looked at from the point of view of the ruling classes, the *Ausgleich* had meant that they had won their war of independence against Vienna. Hungary became an equal partner with Austria within the monarchy. Worsted in the deal were the working people of the country, above all the peasantry, who had made the greatest sacrifice in the fight for freedom and had expected an improvement of their lot from the changes. Double losers were the ethnic populations representing the majority of the country's inhabitants, who simply did not exist in terms of the constitution. The 1848 revolution had begun in the spirit of national independence and complete equality before the law. The settlement merely gave Hungary's dependent status a better name and the Hungarians the consciousness of ascendancy and privileges within the one-thousand-year-old borders. This consciousness was enough to produce a hypertrophic national pride in all those benefiting from the contradictory social changes: in the bourgeoisie, who were quickly growing rich and imitating the aristocracy in all things, and in the middle classes, which were no less keen on aping the gentry. This overwrought pride wanted to find a material outlet, as it were, in the capital. A special occasion offered itself for this when in 1896 the country was preparing to celebrate its millennium of existence.

The Hungarian millennial celebrations thus assumed a peculiar character, tragicomical and grotesque, not unlike the elite Hungarian *Belle Epoque* which it heralded. Anyone realistically assessing the one-thousand years could only find one thing to celebrate: the fact that Hungary, and within it Budapest, had managed to survive at all. From time immemorial the site of the Hungarian capital had been one of the busiest crossing points, which means that it had always been inhabited, with a town having stood here for upwards of two thousand years; but this also meant that the place had always been a destructively "draughty" one, too. The Romans' rich city was laid waste by the waves of the Migration, and the 13th century Mongol invasion left medieval Pest and Buda in ruins in its destructive wake. In the 14th century Buda was again mentioned among the three largest and most beautiful cities in Europe. Humanist culture and Renaissance art first struck root outside Italy in King Matthias's wonderful palace. Just one telling fact, in passing, of the subsequent disasters: after the expulsion of the Turks from Hungary, the number of inhabitants of the three cities of Pest, Buda and Óbuda had dwindled to a mere 500. Commercial Pest with its craftsmen's guilds, military and administrative Buda and agricultural Óbuda were raised on charred ruins almost from nothing during the 18th century.

Now, the illusionary, optimistic mentality of the millennium was wilfully deceiving itself by making this tragic history — splendid precisely in its tragedy, because it proved the nation's vitality and viability after so many set-backs — glitteringly glorious. It only remembered the victorious battles of the lost wars, the brief spells of splendour; it recalled only the glory of the banners, and from all this dream-stuff a cheaply romantic heroic epic concocted itself in place of stark historical reality.

This tawdry and fanciful heroic epic became pretty much part and parcel of the renewed Budapest. The left-bank city had a charming Baroque nucleus. The over-ambitious replanning of the city presumably found it much too unpretentious, and it was wiped out almost without a trace. Its memory is preserved by merely one or two spared buildings — and the photographs of Klösz. Here, the town planners had their weighty arguments concerning transport policy. On the other hand, it is much harder to explain why pseudo-Romanesque ornaments had to be erected on Castle Hill, why the ancient Coronation Church had to be restored in flamboy-ant Gothic style, what megalomania is embodied in the Houses of Parliament on the Danube Embankment, which would have been conveniently big enough for the legislative body of a truly democratic world power, let alone a small country in which only a fraction of the population had the right to vote. It is hard to under-stand why a bigger and more splendid royal palace outbidding even the Viennese Burg had to be erected (and for this purpose a sizable bit stuck on to the hill itself) for a king who stayed rather infrequently in Buda-pest, and even when he did, he had his drinking water brought straight from Vienna to a city famous for its mineral springs. And all this while the authentic, beautiful remnants of the medieval palace and its magnifi-cent earthworks were buried and covered up and the historic monuments and artistic fragments of the build-ings and their authentic medieval carved stones and frescoes in the Castle district were hidden away under plas-ter ornaments to make them look more imposing. Once again, genuine history, the authentic past, did not seem distinguished enough.

Yet another devastation — that of the 1944—1945 siege — had to come for the genuine values to be brought to light from under the gypsum and plaster. The uncovering was then completed by many years of careful restora-tion work. The unique worth of the historic monuments of the Castle Hill lies precisely in the fact that almost every single building reveals to us the layers that bear witness to the destructions and reconstructions of seven or eight centuries.

Of course, it would be very unjust to mention nothing but this. Besides the general flaunting, a good deal of constructive and creative intention was at work as well. The Danube bridges were built one after the other, each of them setting a new technological record in their times, spanning, as they did, the second longest and broadest river in Europe. The embankment was built along the entire city stretch of the river, which, in its material and technical achievements and aesthetic appearance, remains an enduring asset of the city.

The street known today as Népköztársaság útja (People's Republic Avenue. formerly Sugár út), which is certainly one of Europe's most attractive city roads, was also built at this time. Radiating from its downtown origins and moving all the way to the district of villas off the City Park, it has well-laid-out and well-planned transitions and proportions, and with its buildings constructed mostly of fine materials, it is indeed a triumph of city engineering. (The one blemish it has is that, lacking an outward extension as a highway, nor having one in the direction of the Danube, it has never become a real arterial thoroughfare.)

The first underground railway of the continent was also constructed at this time. As well as the cogwheel railway on Széchenyi Hill, with a grade difference of 259 metres on its not quite three-kilometre-long tracks, representing the third technological achievement of its kind in the world. The cable railway up the fifty-degree slope of Castle Hill was also built. And grotesque though the Houses of Parliament might seem compared to their functional significance, it must be admitted that they are the work of an excellent architect and are an impressive example of the Neo-Gothic style. Their technical facilities were well in advance of their age, and still functioning perfectly. Furthermore, with its eighty-eight external statues, internal sculptures, murals, paintings, ornaments, and fine-quality materials, the Parliament is an edifice that has justly become one of the symbols of Budapest.

Parallel with the internal semi-circular boulevard which had earlier developed along the ancient city walls, the more than four-kilometre-long Great Boulevard came into existence. As at the construction of Sugár út, this time, too, overcrowded, unhealthy slums were cleared away. To give an idea of the scale of the project: during the building of the Great Boulevard, roughly the same number of houses had to be pulled down as were erected in their place (251 demolitions, 253 new buildings), but the cubic space of the new buildings was nine times as great as that of the old ones. The new thoroughfare and its tributaries were bound to organize around them completely new large residential districts. Parallel with the building construction, Budapest's basic utility systems, including sewage and water supply, were laid out essentially during these decades. By the end of the century, nearly half a thousand kilometre of gas lines were laid down, carrying fifty million cubic metres of gas daily to the consumers and for public lighting. Also in the same period started regular electricity supply. A good part of the largest Budapest hospitals (János, István, Margit, László) and university polyclinics, still functioning today, were also built at that time. It was then that Budapest's central railway station was constructed, and it was in 1883 that the most important transcontinental express train, the Orient Express, began its first voyage from Budapest. This quarter of a century also saw the replacement of horse tramways and later of steam-powered city trains by electric trams, whose network gradually extended to cover the outskirts of the city. And I could continue the enumeration with the establishment and construction of elementary, secondary and high schools. So, while maintaining our earlier criticism, we must finally pay tribute to that age, to its planners and builders.

Even today, when there is little cause to complain about the rate of development, when we have a modern prefabricated housing technology, tower cranes and machinery with the aid of which some twenty thousand flats are built annually in Budapest—even today, it is difficult to recall our great-grandfathers' feverish building activity. A magic circle was set spinning at an accelerating tempo: the constructions and public works attracted huge masses of people into the capital; the increased population required more and more living space and catering establishments; the construction stepped up the development of a whole series of industries which in turn demanded even more manpower: the complicated system of big-city services which demanded another substantial increase in the labour force came into existence. Capital could find no more securely profitable investment in the given circumstances than real estate. And no matter how much was invested in real estate property, it seemed that its value and profitability went soaring up, since every square metre of dwelling space found an eager customer. If we consider that the one-time suburb, which today is the 7th district and forms part of the city's nucleus with one-hundred thousand people to a hectare, was built in a mere two years, we can better appreciate why the nickname "Chicago" attaches to it to this day. Yet this part, like the entire city centre, was built brick upon brick, and the mortar was still carried in four-handled pans to the scaffolding by multi-skirted peasant girls from the Buda Hills. And let's add: the houses, roads, sewage conduits and other public works, as well as the wonderful bridges, were built by people who lived mostly on bread and onions, bread and pickled cucumbers, or at best, on bread and lard. It would be really difficult to form an idea of the range of social conditions in millennial Hungary were it not for the buildings which tell a story about these conditions. The blocks of flats were generally designed to have a narrow front facing the street, with the landlord's residence on the first floor. On the other floors facing the street, other more or less confortable, spacious flats with bathrooms and maid's rooms were made; but more than two-thirds of the flats looked on the inner courtyard, and on this side the kitchen doors of the one-room and kitchen flats were aligned along the *gang* or passage-way running round the whole length of the courtyard-side of the house. The latter was the typical Budapest flat, two-thirds of the flats being of this kind, and the majority of these room-and-kitchen flats even lacked the convenience of lavatories and bathrooms.

The bourgeoisie had both the incentive and inclination to build. They were growing rich in those years, and so they had the means as well. Yet, strangely enough, they failed to develop their own specific style. It is a malady we have in common with most European cities, but ours was compounded with the delusion of grandeur that we have mentioned above. Much like a new love affair *à la* Stendhal contrives a past for itself, the bourgeoisie also wanted to build itself an "authentic" past, although its own genuine one was nothing to be ashamed of. Having feathered its nest, it longed for a different past and thus brought about a "heraldic" architecture in what is known as eclecticism. The fronts of the overcrowded tenements with courtyards were cast in the image of Baroque mansions and Renaissance palaces. The balcony of the landlord was supported by colossal Herculeses, and though much mocked at by the authors of the period, it was the 1944—1945 siege that showed up their tragi-comic character best, when these hollow plaster Herculeses dangled from the balconies on a few pitiful wires in the wind.

However, the bizarre forms were embodied in some finer material, force of habit has helped out, and taste has become buttressed by piety: the well-nigh one hundred years have lent a certain patina to eclecticism, too. Not only the contemporary public buildings but also some of the dwelling houses (e.g., a few of the eclectic houses of the Great Boulevard) have been placed under protection. "Secession" or *art nouveau* appeared in Hungary in the 1890s and ran parallel with eclecticism, and the neo-Baroque it embodied, for a long time. Both styles had outstanding representatives in Hungary. To mention but two of the very talented designers: Imre Steindl, the architect of the Houses of Parliament, the new Town Hall, the University on Museum Boulevard, the parish church in Elizabeth district and innumerable private palaces; and Ödön Lechner, responsible for the Museum of Applied Arts, the Geophysical Institute, and the Postal Savings Bank, who sought some kind of national style and thought he had found this new idiom—and this is again characteristic of the period—partly in decorative folk motifs alien to architecture, partly in some never-existing Far Eastern national past.

There is a striking oddity which is in some way connected with imitation in the town's structure itself. The greatest asset of Budapest is undoubtedly her wonderful situation, and the most scenic part is obviously the Buda hills from where this situation can be viewed and enjoyed to the best advantage. Nevertheless, the Pest bourgeoisie had its respectable middle-class quarters built in the eastern plain. The Buda slopes were appreciated to some extent, and a few summer villas did crop up there from the mid-19th century on, but it was not developed as a residential quarter until much later. This applies even to the fairly central Rózsadomb (Hill of Roses), which became even more easily accessible after the construction of Margaret Bridge.

We have seen how the city tried to slough off its original skin, how it was set on building itself a pseudo-tradition, and what models it wanted to emulate with great effort. In the end, the Budapest that emerged by the turn of the century had become a magnificent city with an atmosphere all her own. Why? Was it merely her situation that was responsible for her unique, unmistakable character? Of course, it was that, too. But beyond all that, it was its inhabitants and their way of life.

If we regard *fin de siècle*-Budapest as a little multinational America within Hungary to which those on the fringe of existence began to flock in large numbers to try their luck or at least to make a living, the comparison is an appropriate one. Oddly enough, the United States is in fact a slow-working "melting pot" in comparison with Budapest. Here, the levelling process needed much less time to be completed.

Like other trading towns lying on the crossroads of the four points of the compass, Pest and Buda were at all times multi-lingual. Pest was founded by the Ismaelites, that is, Mohammedan eastern Bulgarians; in Buda the "Italians" (a cover term for neo-Latin peoples) had their own street in medieval times, and so had the Jews; the Germans and Hungarians had separate parishes; and Southern Slavs fleeing from the advancing Turks founded Rátz or Serb Town, known as the Tabán. As mentioned earlier, by the 18th century only a few hundred people lived in the three towns. Resettlement was for a long time controlled by an imperial decree in terms of which house plots could only be allocated to persons whose mother tongue was German and who belonged to the Catholic faith. Although evaded from the start, the decree was not revoked until the end of the century

The first major breakthrough occurred at the beginning of the last century. In the German-speaking towns of what was to become Budapest, there arose the national centre of Hungarian culture with high schools, the Academy of Sciences, public collections, theatres, literary societies and publishing ventures. The real change, however, was brought about by the accelerating capitalism which followed upon the unification of the city.

But there was a special factor which encouraged the Budapest bourgeoisie to adopt Hungarian ways, namely, the city had to win its independent political and economic status in face of Vienna. The majority of this stratum was still German-speaking in 1880 or at least could use German as well as native speakers. It was in their vital interest to *want* to become Hungarians in the spirit of the nationalism that went hand in hand with capitalism. The striving for political and economic independence brought with it an adoptive choice of nationality. There was wide-spread campaigning at institutes of higher education for Hungarian to be the language of instruction, and in these campaigns foreigners as well as Hungarians were taking part. Where not long before, the Hungarian-language press enjoyed at most a stunted growth, now Hungarian dailies and weeklies sprang up and began to prosper. (We are moved to smile as we read these papers, not because of their antiquated style or outlook, but because the language shows that a good many of the authors were really thinking in German, they were not "to the manner born", and the language they were using was only their adopted means of communication. The press played a major role in the city becoming Hungarianized as well as in creating a specific Pest dialect and adding one other to the local forms of speech, which was to meet with a lot of objections later, and not without good reason, on the part of Hungarians with a sense of linguistic propriety.)

It was a different matter with the Hungarianization of the lower strata and the working class. Industry, in default of a local labour supply, invited skilled workers from more developed areas of Europe, Bohemia and Moravia in particular, as well as from further afield. The numerous contingents of unskilled workers, or day-labourers, as they used to be called then, flocked to the capital from the Great Plain, from the Slav and Rumanian settled peripheries. Linguistic colonies were formed; mass was celebrated in several languages, the publications of the incipient labour movement appeared in several languages, the meetings were addressed in several languages.

Here, as elsewhere in the world, the decisive factor was the need for the polyglot working force to have a common means of communication, which naturally became the language of the majority. (By the way, this language became a specific dialect in so far as it used German words bent to Hungarian for naming machine parts, tools and work processes, but it remained basically Hungarian in its phonology and syntax.) Apparently some part was played in this assimilation by the big-hearted tolerance, or instinctive liberalism, that the people of Pest, hailing from all parts of the compass, had evidenced from the start. The least pressure, moral or otherwise, would have met with resistance. By the end of the century, multi-lingualism had disappeared spontaneously even from the workers' movement, there being no need for it any more.

Traces of multi-lingualism did persist for a long time to come in one quarter of the town, in Óbuda, and here and there among the old. But by and large, the Hungarianization of the city had clearly run its course by the beginning of this century. We know of one specific fact indicative of the change in this connection, namely, that when the German Theatre in Pest burnt down in 1887, no new project was born for its reconstruction. Merely two generations ago, most Hungarian-language theatrical ventures failed in Pest-Buda, with only a few of them being barely kept alive by an enthusiastic minority. And now, when there was a genuine theatrical boom, not a single German company could survive.

Owing to their origins, lot and pioneering character, the people of Pest lacked the fanaticism of prejudice. Consequently, they were often castigated as sceptical and of a frivolous cast of mind. True, the Budapesters watched and interpreted life with a characteristic irony and self-irony, under the very nose of official bigotry and fanaticism. Their acid criticism imparted a strange, acrid taste to every idea and ideal. Yet the civil and labour rights campaigns of the age are proof that while never missing a chance to make a joke, even about the most serious matters, day in and day out, these people were able to take serious matters seriously, and if need be, to lay down their lives for a just cause. Scepticism and responsibility were simultaneously present in their wry irony and self-mockery.

Appearances often did bear out the charge of frivolousness. The extreme social range and the uncertainty of existence would explain and excuse that charge, too! But in a large measure it was that the way of life, despite the intentions of the architects to give Budapest a Western look, pulled the city towards a Mediterranean direction. The Budapester—although the climate makes it possible only to a limited extent—lives in the street, in the open. The coffee-houses were mushrooming all over the city and some of them came out onto the pavement. It is hard to understand today, and contemporary records were equally puzzled, that the coffee-houses only a block away from one another were full at all hours of the day. (And how come that the proprietors were able to make their shops become paying concerns when most of their patrons sat at their tables for hours by a cup of coffee and a glass of water?) Ritual promenades sprang up in the City Park, on Margaret Island and along certain other roads that filled with strollers and gazers at particular hours of the day, bad weather notwithstanding. (For a long time crowds promenaded even on the frozen Danube, the bold promenaders being watched by crowds on the shore until, following an accident involving many people, the police banned this form of amusement.) Promenading and sitting in the cafés belonged to living in the open, in public. The papers were read and commented on here, and politics were discussed here. What electronics does for us these days, the café and the promenade did then, for they functioned as the rallying force of the mass media. One might add that they were scarcely slower in spreading, commenting upon and shaping public opinion than radio or television are now. In a country stagnating in feudalism, in a municipal country that was semi-dependent and backward, Budapest thus became the centre where the people did not think in parochial but in national and European terms, that is, in terms of international politics.

It is, I think, unnecessary to emphasize how all this attracted Hungarian cultural life, how the city became the undisputed seat of the nation's cultural wealth, the unchallenged centre of the entire country's cultural and intellectual life.

In case anyone should accuse me of one-sided local patriotism, I must hasten to add that *fin de siècle*-Budapest soon overtook and even surpassed its own models in moral defects.

The youths of the aristocracy and bourgeoisie wanted to sow their wild oats and have a roaring good time, and though many a fortune that was reaped at home was dissipated in West European gambling houses and brothels, the entrepreneur spirit of the Budapest bourgeoisie strove to create ample local opportunities for this kind of extravagant spending at home. We have already mentioned that there never had been as many theatres in Budapest as in those years. But were they really theatres? The word applied to most of them as a euphemism only. For the most part they were show-business establishments of a more or less cheap kind, which acted as a natural buyer's market for the prettier girls of the agricultural and the urban proletariat who were produced by domestic misery in such prodigious supply that the surplus could be exported. That the underworld pursued its games in a mild manner can, to some extent, be regarded as a Budapest speciality. By international standards security in the city was not bad, and the few violent crimes that occurred never failed to make a big stir. There arose as a special and typical Budapest form of criminal offence the intellectual crime: the resourcefulness of imposture and sharp practices seemed to be fathomless. In the period in question, the forging of bills was the order of the day, and the sure way out in case of discovery in the smart circles was a bullet through the head or a boat for America.

All things considered, it is honestly not some nostalgic longing for the *Belle Epoque* which makes us in Budapest think back to the last twenty years of the 19th and the early years of the present century with a certain emotional respect, despite their grotesque oddities and crimes. For we must remember that the new uniform municipal administration united in 1873 three provincial-like towns. Most of the houses were single-storey ones; the roads were unpaved, the garbage was carted away, if it in fact was, by convicts; drinking water was delivered to the houses in carts and barrows with cries of "Donauwasser!" Where the Great Boulevard is today the backwater of the Danube meandered sluggishly and was used to water cabbage-patches, while at either end of the future Boulevard there were the not at all safe hide-outs of ragamuffins. Yet, at the turn of the century here stood a large city of one million inhabitants, complete with public utilities, electric supply, five bridges, paved roads, lively traffic, developed industry—one of Europe's modern metropolises.

The chronicler of these changes is György Klösz and his photographs. Had he photographed the buildings only, it would have been no mean thing; the townscape has changed a good deal in the intervening one hundred years, and his photographs preserve quite a lot of what no longer exists. But—and here lies the special value of these photographs in contrast to the earlier lithographs—some of them capture spontaneously, almost accidentally, the people of the streets of Budapest. True, they are not the politicians, the members of the National Casino, nor the smart set of the promenade of the Inner City. They would never have posed for Klösz's machine. Nor did they walk about or stand around during the sunlit hours of the day. Those who people these photographs are shoemakers, journeymen, tradesmen, maids off to the market, workers, the common folk: the very men and women who brought this sudden change about with the daily labour of their hands.

On the previous page:
View of Castle Hill from Ferenc József (now Roosevelt)
Square at the turn of the century.

Warehouse of the Danube Steamship Co. on the Ferenc József (now Belgrád) Embankment. In the background, the tiny houses of the Tabán are visible on the slope of Gellért Hill, *c.* 1890.

On the slope of Gellért Hill in the one-time Tabán, *c.* 1890. This quarter was pulled down in 1932–1933.

On the next page:
The regulation and levelling of Szarvas (Deer) Square in 1894.

On the previous page:
The Tabán, Krisztinaváros (Christina Town) and the
Castle from Gellért Hill in the 1890s.

Townscape from Krisztinaváros with the former Karátsonyi Palace, pulled down in 1938. The 1870s.
(Photo by unknown photographer.)

The ball-room in the Karátsonyi Palace, 1900.
The staircase in the Karátsonyi Palace.
The Karátsonyi Palace in the place of the building at
55, Krisztina Boulevard, c. 1900.
The concert-room of the Karátsonyi Palace.
The picture gallery of the Karátsonyi Palace.

On the next page:
The Dísz tér (Parade Square) in the Castle District
with Úri Street on the left and Tárnok Street on the
right, c. 1890.

The one time Marczibányi House on Dísz tér (Parade Square), in the place of the present "Muskétás" Restaurant, c. 1900.

Országház Street in the second half of the 1890s. The buildings visible still stand, though in a somewhat altered form. (Photo by an unknown photographer.)

The northern side of Szentháromság (Holy Trinity) Square with Fortuna Street on the right and the monument of the Holy Trinity on the left, *c.* 1900.

The Mary Magdalene Church (formerly the "garrison" church) on Kapisztrán Square, *c.* 1900. The building was severely damaged during the Second World War. It was pulled down in the 1950s, but its tower was kept and restored.

Demolition of the old Bécsi-kapu (Vienna Gate) in 1896. The new gate was constructed in the same place and in the same form in 1936.

On the next page:
The Royal Palace of Buda before its reconstruction at the turn of the century, with the "astle Bazaar" below, *c.* 1895.

A room in the Royal Palace, c. 1895. (Photo by Mór Erdélyi.)

A festive procession starting from the courtyard of the Royal Palace on 5th June, 1896.

The one-time stairway to the central part of the Royal Palace of Buda from the garden, c. 1900.

A view of Pest from the Várkert (Castle Garden), c. 1910. In front of the terrace, Eugene of Savoy's statue (still standing today) is visible. (Photo by unknown photographer.)

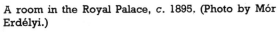

Terminal of the Sváb (now Szabadság) Mountain cog-wheel railway in the Városmajor district, *c.* 1896.

The cog-wheel railway in the 1890s.

On the next page:
View of Víziváros (Water Town) from Castle Hill, *c.* 1900.

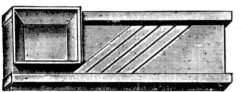

Tobacconist's shop at the turn of the century. (Photo by unknown photographer.)

The western side of Bomba (now Batthyány) Square with the steeple of St. Anna's Church on the left, *c.* 1895. (Photo by unknown photographer.)

On the next page:
The Lukács and Császár baths with the Rózsadomb (Hill of Roses) in the background, *c.* 1894. (Photo by unknown photographer.)

Interior of the Rácfürdő (Serbian Baths), c. 1900.

The Hotel Császárfürdő (Emperor's Baths), c. 1900.
(Photo by Stengel Co., Dresden.)

Interior of the Rácfürdő (Serbian Baths).

On the previous page:
The Víziváros (Water Town) seen from Castle Hill, with Margaret Bridge and Margaret Island in the background, c. 1890.

Access to Margaret Island from Margaret Bridge in the early 1900s. (Photo by Mór Erdélyi.)

Waterfall on Margaret Island, c. 1890. In those days, the water ran straight into the Danube.

Group photograph from the turn of the century.

Margaret Island was often flooded by subsoil water.
On such occasions, people walked on plank-ways.
(Photo by unknown photographer.)

Margaret Island in the 1890s.

On the next page:
The Újpest embankment and the surroundings of
Pozsonyi Road seen from Margaret Island, *c.* 1900.

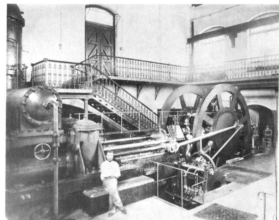

In a baking plant, *c.* 1896.

Workshop interior, *c.* 1900.

The engine-house of the old waterworks in Pest where Parliament building stands today on Kossuth Lajos Square, in the 1880s.

Factory yard, *c.* 1890.

A workshop in the Láng factory in the 1900s. (Photo by unknown photographer.)

The Rudolf (now Széchenyi) Embankment. On the extreme right of the picture, the construction of the Parliament building, c. 1895, (Photo by unknown photographer.)

The Margaret Bridge, *c.* 1900.

View of the former Lipótváros (Leopold Town), *c.* 1900.

The Houses of Parliament, *c.* 1900.

Országház (now Kossuth Lajos) Square, *c.* 1900. (Photo by Mór Erdélyi.)

The roof-raising ceremony of Parliament on May 5, 1894. (Photo by Károly Divald.)

Carrying the Hungarian crown to the Houses of Parliament, on the occasion of the opening of the first National Assembly held in the new building on June 8 1896.

The vicinity of the Houses of Parliament, c. 1895.

The king of Siam with his entourage in front of the Houses of Parliament, c. 1900. (Photo by unknown photographer.)

The former Palace of Justice (today the Ethnographic Museum) with Alkotmány (Constitution) Street on the right, c. 1900.

Alkotmány Street, c. 1900. In the background, the Váci Boulevard (now Bajcsy-Zsilinszky Road) and, on the left, a Unitarian church.

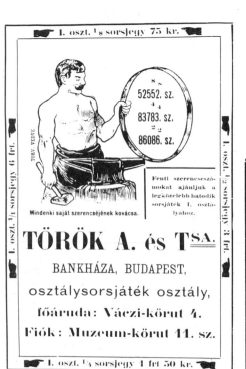

The Újépület barracks, seen from the top of the Parliament buildings. In 1898 it was pulled down and Szabadság (Liberty) Square was built in its place. (Photo by unknown photographer.)

The Produce and Stock Exchange (today the headquarters of Hungarian Television) on Szabadság Square, c. 1905.

View of Szabadság Square from the dome of St. Stephen's Basilica. On the right, the headquarters of the Austro-Hungarian (later National) Bank, and on the left, the Stock Exchange, both under construction. (Photo by Czettel and Deutsch.)

Ferenc József (now Roosevelt) Square with the Coronation Hill, which was demolished in 1877, in the middle. In the background, the building of the Hungarian Academy of Sciences, *c.* 1868.

The Pest abutment of the Lánchíd (Chain Bridge) seen from the Coronation Hill, *c.* 1868.

Ferenc József Square, with the Academy of Sciences in the background, *c.* 1890.

The Gresham Palace on Ferenc József Square, *c.* 1907.

On the next page:
The tram terminal on the Rudolf (now Széchenyi) Embankment near the Academy of Sciences, *c.* 1895.

One of the warehouses of the Danube Steamship Company at the Pest abutment of the Lánchíd (Chain Bridge), *c.* 1900. (Photo by unknown photographer.)

Gellért Hill seen from the Ferenc József (Belgrád) Embankment, with the one-time Sáros Baths on the left, *c.* 1895.

Paying toll at the Pest abutment of the Lánchíd, *c.* 1910. (Photo by J. Müllner (?).)

On the next page:
Ferenc József (now Roosevelt) Square seen from the Academy, *c.* 1895.

Lassan hajts!

The Vigadó (Municipal Concert Hall) with the Thonet Court on the left. At the end of Vigadó Street, the vista of Gizella (now Vörösmarty) Square, and in front of the Vigadó, the Hangli kiosk, c. 1900.

The great hall of the Vigadó, c. 1870. (Photo by Béla Gévay.)

The staircase of the Vigadó. (Photo by Béla Gévay.)

The Pest embankment of the Danube between the Petőfi Square and the Vigadó. From right to left, the Greek Orthodox Church can be seen in the square, the Hotel Bristol and the Hotel Hungaria on the embankment, c. 1910.

Dining hall in the 1890s of the Hotel Hungaria, built in 1869 and demolished in 1945. Today the Hotel Duna-Inter-Continental stands in its place.

On the previous page:
View of the Danube from the Ferenc József (now Belgrád) Embankment. In the background the Gellért Hill and the Royal Palace with the Matthias Church whose tower, under construction, dates the picture to about 1894.

Interior of the Inner City Parish Church in Pest, *c.* 1895.

The Inner City Paris Church with the old Piarist grammar school on the left, and the Town Hall (pulled down in 1900), *c.* 1895.

The Inner City Parish Church seen from Váci Street with the supporting wall necessitated by the construction of Elizabeth Bridge, *c.* 1900.

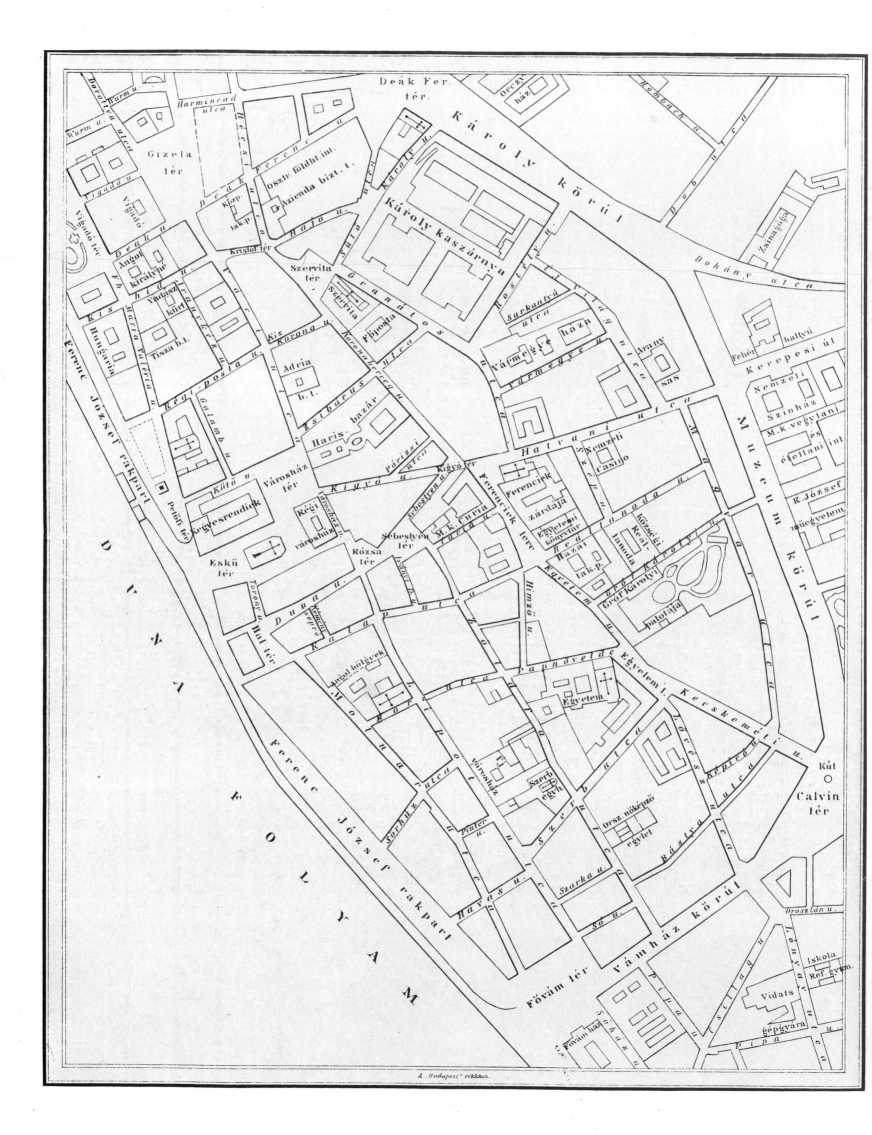

A „Budapest" cikkhez.

The Inner City in 1893. Contemporary map.

The Inner City parsonage, which was pulled down in the course of town-planning operations during the construction of Elizabeth Bridge, c. 1890.

On the next page:
The Kígyó (now Felszabadulás) Square with the two Klotild Palaces, between them the Elizabeth Bridge under construction, 1902. (Photo by Mór Erdélyi.)

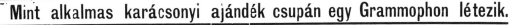

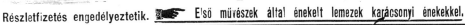

The former Párisi udvar (Paris Court) in the place of the present court, *c.* 1900. (Photo by unknown photographer.)

The Brudern House in Kígyó (Snake) Street, which included the former Párisi udvar, *c.* 1900.

Hatvani (now Kossuth Lajos) Street, c. 1880, before
street widening was begun in the 1890s, with the
Franciscan Church on the right.

The Franciscan Church with Hatvani (now Kossuth
Lajos) Street on the left and the Ferenciek tere
(Franciscan Square, now Károlyi Mihály Street) on the
right, c. 1880. (Photo by unknown photographer.)

The Dreher Palace on the corner of Hatvani and Gránátos (now Városház) Streets in the 1880s.

In front of the Dreher Palace.

The building at 2, Semmelweis Street, on the corner of Semmelweis and Hatvani (now Kossuth Lajos) Streets.

A hall in the palace of the National Casino at 5, Hatvani Street in the 1890s. The building was damaged during the Second World War and was subsequently pulled down.

On the next pages:
The kiosk on Erzsébet (now Engels) Square in the 1890s.

Deák Ferenc Square in the 1880s.

Bécsi (Vienna) Street seen from Szervita (now Marti-
nelli) Square, c. 1895.

The Haas Palace on Gizella (now Vörösmarty) Square,
c. 1900.

View of Gizella Square from Harmincad Street.

The Gerbeaud (now Vörösmarty) confectionery, *c.* 1900.

Gizella (now Vörösmarty) Square, *c.* 1890.

Exit and entrance to the Gizella Square underground railway terminal, *c.* 1900. (Photo by unknown photographer.)

Building the underground railway terminal on Gizella Square. Photo taken on May 6, 1895.

Bookshop on the corner of Váci Street and Kishíd (now Türr István) Street, c. 1890. (Photo by unknown photographer.)

Koronaherceg (now Petőfi Sándor) Street seen from Hatvani (now Kossuth Lajos) Street in the 1890s. (Photo by unknown photographer.)

The corner of Kristóf Square and Váci Street with the statue of Saint Christopher, seen from Gizella (now Vörösmarty) Square, in the 1890s.

Detail of Váci Street seen from Gizella (now Vörösmarty) Square in the 1890s, with the old Town Hall in the background.

Váci Street seen from Eskü (Oath) Square in the 1890s.

The market place on Városház Square in the 1890.s

The former Városház (Town Hall) Square with the
old Town Hall, pulled down in 1900, in the 1890s.
(Presently the site of the Faculty of Philosophy of the
Eötvös Loránd University.)

Jöjjön velem

az élet mysteriumaiba, megtanitom arra, hogy mikép védekezzék leghatalmasabb ellenségei ellen.

The former Kígyó Pharmacy on Kígyó (now Felszabadulás) Square, pulled down at the time of the construction of Elizabeth Bridge.

On the previous page:
Hal (Fish) Square, built around the turn of the century, with Kalap (now Irányi) Street in the back ground, c. 1895.

Duna (Danube) Street seen from the Danube in the 1890s. In the background, the tower of the Franciscan Church. In the course of town-planning operations in the inner city, during the construction of Elizabeth Bridge, this part of the street was pulled down.

This hotel stood in front of the present house at 27, Belgrád Embankment, with the Fish Square behind. Photo taken from the direction of the Danube, c. 1895.

On the next pages:
Courtyard on the corner of the former Torony (Tower) and Duna (Danube) Streets, with the steeple of the Inner City Church in the background, c. 1895.

The corner of Torony and Duna Streets, c. 1895.

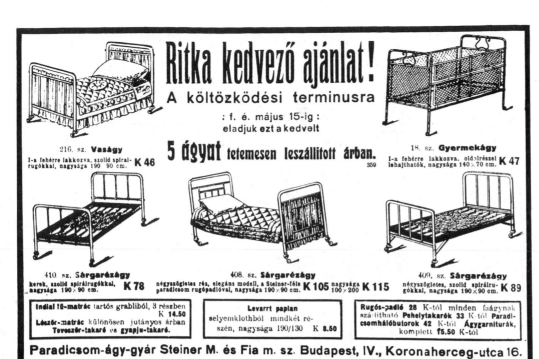
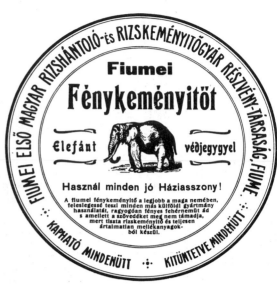

Szerb (Serb) Street seen from Egyetem (University) Square, c. 1896.

Detail of Lipót (now Váci) Street with St. Michael's Church of the Mary Ward's nuns, c. 1895. (Photo by unknown photographer.)

Interior of St. Michael's Church (47, Váci Street).

The one-time Rózsa (Rose) Square and Lipót Street with St. Michael's Church of the Mary Ward's nuns, c. 1895.

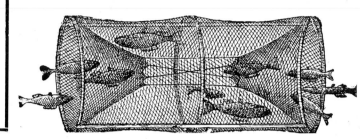

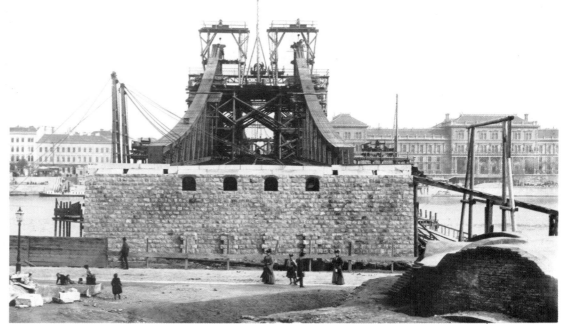

On the previous pages:
Kecskeméti Street seen from Calvin Square, c. 1895.

View of the Danube from the Gellért Embankment with the Fővámpalota (Main Customs House, today Karl Marx University of Economics) on the left, c. 1890.

The Danube embankment in the place of Szabadság (Liberty) Bridge. On the right, on the Pest bank, the Main Customs House, in the background, the tower of the Calvinist Church on Calvin Square, c. 1895.

The Buda abutment of the Ferenc József (later Szabadság or Liberty) Bridge under construction in 1896.

Detail of the embankment at the Main Customs House, c. 1893, prior to the building of Ferenc József Bridge (1895–1896).

On the next page:
The Ferenc József (later Szabadság or Liberty) Bridge with the market place on the embankment, in 1896.

Calvin Square and the Hungarian National Museum, *c.* 1880.

Calvin Square, *c.* 1898, with the Danubius Well in the middle, which was set up on Engels Square in 1957.

The National Riding-hall, *c.* 1880, on the present Pollack Mihály Square. Today the headquarters of the Hungarian Radio stand on this site.

Count Alajos Károlyi's palace on the corner of today's Pollack Mihály Square and Múzeum Street, with the National Riding-hall, destroyed in the Second World War, on the left, *c.* 1880.

The garden of Count Alajos Károlyi's palace, *c.* 1880.

"The Daughter of the Nabob of Dolova", National Theatre, 1893.

"The Prodigal Son", People's Theatre, 1891.

The company of the National Theatre round 1885. On the extreme left, with a book in his hand, Ede Paulay, director of the theatre. (Photo by unknown photographer.)

The former building of the National Theatre at 3, Rákóczi Road in the 1900s, with the Hotel Pannonia, today a student hostel.

On the next page:
The Paris department store, *c.* 1900, at 38–40, Kerepesi (now Rákóczi) Road. On August 24, 1903, a short-circuit caused a fire which destroyed the store.

KLEIN és BÄUMEL

...LEIN és BAUMEL
A és VIASZKGYERTYA GYÁRA

66 NŐI KALAP DIVAT TEREM 66

KLEIN és BÄUMEL
CZUKORKA VIASZKGYERTYA GYÁRA · CANDITEN WACHSKERZEN FABRIK

On the previous pages:

The St. Roch (now Semmelweis) Hospital, c. 1890.
The "Immaculata" statue in front of it has been pulled
down.

The Népszínház (People's Theatre) on Blaha Lujza
Square in the 1890s. In the background on the left,
Népszínház Sreet.

The house at 66, Kerepesi (now Rákóczi) Road, c.
1895. The shops in it were converted from a jail.

The courtyard of the house at 66, Kerepesi Road,
c. 1895. Until the end of the 1880s, it was the scene
of executions.

Detail of the courtyard.

Portal and shop windows at the turn of the century. (Photos by unknown photographer.)

On the next page:
Market place on Újvásár (now Köztársaság or Republic) Square in the 1890s. (Photo by Mór Erdélyi.)

The Baross Café on József Boulevard, *c.* 1895.

The Józsefváros (Joseph Town) parish church on Mária Terézia (now Horváth Mihály) Square, *c.* 1900.

The Rákóczi Square market hall, *c.* 1900.

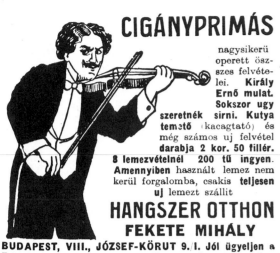

The beginning of József Boulevard at the People's Theatre, *c.* 1895.

Népszínház (People's Theatre) Street, *c.* 1895, with the People's Theatre in the background.

Authors and actors in the Dohány (Tobacco) Street garden of the "Otthon" (Home) circle of writers and journalists, c. 1908. (Photo by Mór Erdélyi.)

The junction of József and Erzsébet (now Lenin) Boulevards at Kerepesi (now Rákóczi) Road, c. 1896, with the People's Theatre on the left and the New York Palace in the middle.

Game-room of the New York (now Hungária) Café, c. 1896.

The New York Café

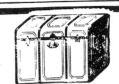

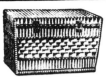

On the previous pages:
Erzsébet (now Lenin) Boulevard from Kerepesi (now Rákóczi) Road, *c.* 1894.

The Oktogon (now November 7 Square) and Teréz (now Lenin) Boulevard towards the Western Railroad Station, *c.* 1896.

The Western Railroad Station under construction, *c.* 1877. (Photo by unknown photographer.)

The Western Railroad Station at the end of the 1870s.

The Western Railroad Station, *c.* 1896.

On the previous pages:
Lipót (now Szt. István) Boulevard. In the middle to right the Vígszínház (Gaiety Theatre) under construction, 1895. Behind the scaffolding, the Rózsadomb (Hill of Roses).

On the next page:
Károly (now Tanács) Boulevard with Dob Street at the right corner; *c.* 1890.

Váci Boulevard (later Vilmos Császár Road, now Bajcsy-Zsilinszky Road) at the end of Andrássy (now Népköztársaság or People's Republic) Avenue, with the Basilica on the left *c.* 1900.

St. Stephen's Basilica, *c.* 1905, just before construction was completed.

The corner of Váci Boulevard (now Bajcsy-Zsilinszky Road) and Hajós Street in the 1880s.

The synagogue in Dohány Street, c. 1890.

The Pekáry House at 47, Király (now Majakovszkij) Street, seen from Nagymező Street, with Csányi Street on the left, c. 1896.

On the next pages:
The market place on István (now Klauzál) Square, c. 1895.

Városligeti (now Gorkij) Avenue, seen from Lövölde (Shooting-gallery) Square in the 1890s.

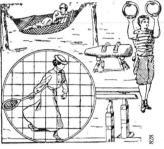
The gymnasium in the Erzsébet girl's school (today Teleki Blanka grammar school) at 37, Ajtósi Dürer Row, in the 1900s.

School-room of the Teleki Blanka grammar school in the 1900s.

Skating rink in the Teleki Blanka grammar school.

The yard of the Teleki Blanka grammar school.

On the next page:
The terminal at Aréna Road (now Dózsa György út) of the horse tramway.

The first bus at the corner of Andrássy Avenue and Vilmos Császár Road (now Népköztársaság útja and Bajcsy-Zsilinszky út), c. 1914.

The Andrássy (now Népköztársaság or People's Republic) Avenue in 1896, at the time of the millennial exhibition, seen from Váci Boulevard (now Bajcsy-Zsilinszky Road). (Photo by Mór Erdélyi.)

The construction of the underground railway on Andrássy Avenue, September 1894.

Construction of the underground railway at the Oktogon (now November 7 Square) in 1894.

The construction of the underground railway with the "Gloriette" drinking fountain in the background. It stood in place of the millennial monument on Hősök tere (Heroes' Square), September 1894.

The Opera House, c. 1900.

In the foreground, Liszt Ferenc Square, on the right Andrássy Avenue with an omnibus. In the background, Jókai Square, c. 1896. (Photo by Mór Erdélyi.)

The Reitter Café in the Drechsler Palace opposite the Opera House, c. 1896.

On the previous page:
Oktogon (now November 7 Square) with a view of the Városliget (City Park). The millennial monument had not yet been set up, *c.* 1890.

Villas on Sugár (later Andrássy, today Népköztársaság or People's Republic) Avenue. The trees on the avenue were newly planted. 1880s.

The building of the School of Design and the Art Teachers' Training School (today's Academy of Fine Arts) on Sugár út, *c.* 1880.

Ornamental fountain in the 1880s.

Shop window of a perfumery at 37, Andrássy Avenue in the 1900s. (Photo by unknown photographer.)

DROGERIA
PARFUMERIA

KET ORO
EISN

KALODONT
legjobb Fog Crème

EISNER GYULA

DROGERIA

MAGYAR és
FRANCZIA
COGNAC

BODECA

DROGERIA

DROGERIA

PASTA

AMERICAN
DRUGGIST

PEBECO

COLGATE'S
DENTAL CREAM

The "Gloriette" drinking fountain in the Városliget (City Park) on what is today Hősök tere (Heroes' Square), in the place of the millennial monument, in the 1880s.

The Art Gallery in 1904–1905. The sculptures flanking the stairs were later placed on the millennial monument.

The Museum of Fine Arts, c. 1906.

The old hall of the skating rink in the Városliget (City Park) in the 1890s.

On the skating rink in the Városliget, c. 1900. (Photo by Mór Erdélyi.)

The pond in the Városliget c. 1910.

The Vajdahunyad Castle and the pond in the Városliget in the 1900s.

On the next page:
In the Városliget (City Park), c. 1900.

The old entrance to the Zoo, c. 1895.

The Aréna Theatre in the Városliget (City Park), c. 1896.

The rotunda erected especially for the painting entitled "The Arrival of the Conquering Magyars" by Árpád Feszty, in the City Park, in the place of the Museum of Fine Arts, c. 1896.

"The Arrival of the Conquering Magyars" under preparation. At the bottom of the ladder, Árpád Feszty, who painted the large-scale panorama with nine other painters, 1894. (Photo by Mór Erdélyi.)

The millennial race ground in May 1896.

Sideshow in the Városliget in the 1910s.

On the previous page:
Part of the Városliget (City Park) in front of the Hall of Industry, *c.* 1896.

Parts of the Millennial Exhibition in the Hall of Industry, 1896.

Inauguration ceremony of the Millennial Exhibition organized on the occasion of the thousandth anniversary of the Magyar Conquest of Hungary, on May 2 1896.

The Hall of Industry.

The Golden Book Pavilion at the Millennial Exhibition. It served for housing a keepsake album ornamented with gold and enamel in which visitors wrote their names.

The Millennial Exhibition in the Hall of Industry.

On the next page :
György Klösz's studio in the Inner City at 1, Hatvani (now Kossuth Lajos) Street, *c.* 1890.